MIDDLE EAST LEADERS™

ANWAR SADAT

Magdalena Alagna

The Rosen Publishing Group, Inc.,
New York

Published in 2004 by The Rosen Publishing Group, Inc.
29 East 21st Street, New York, NY 10010

First Edition

Library of Congress Cataloging-in-Publication Data
Alagna, Magdalena.
Anwar Sadat / by Magdalena Alagna.
     p. cm. — (Middle East leaders)
Summary: Examines the life and leadership skills of Egyptian president Anwar Sadat, who won a Nobel Peace Prize for his role in the peace process after the 1973 war with Israel.
Includes bibliographical references and index.
ISBN 0-8239-4464-6
1. Sadat, Anwar, 1918–1981—Juvenile literature. 2. Presidents—Egypt—Biography—Juvenile literature. [1. Sadat, Anwar, 1918–1981. 2. Presidents—Egypt. 3. Nobel Prizes—Biography.]
I. Title. II. Series.
DT107.85.A43 2003
962.05'4'092—dc21

                                        2003009416

Manufactured in the United States of America

CONTENTS

INTRODUCTION
DREAMING BIG DREAMS

■ In 1977, Egyptian president Anwar Sadat traveled to Washington, D.C. There he worked with President Jimmy Carter and Israeli prime minister Menachem Begin on a peace treaty between Egypt and Israel.

Anwar Sadat was the president of Egypt from 1970 to 1981. His tragic assassination at the hands of fundamentalist Muslims ended his leadership. Sadat was an especially high-profile president because Egypt was one of the leaders of the Arab world. Egypt has the largest population of all the Arab nations. Sadat's speech to the Israeli parliament in 1977 electrified the world because no Egyptian leader had ever done anything like it. Israel and Egypt were sworn enemies, and Sadat went to Israel to talk to Israel's parliament about a peace treaty. In one bold and decisive move toward friendship, Sadat changed events in the Middle East. Anwar Sadat saw the speech as a crucial step toward peace. His visionary act helped to bring about peace between the two nations. It also earned him the 1978 Nobel Peace Prize, which he shared with Israel's prime minister, Menachem Begin.

CHAPTER ONE
LIFE IN MIT ABUL KUM

■ This photograph of a city street looks to be from a European capital. In fact, this is Aiwal Avenue in Cairo, Egypt, in 1937. Egyptian architecture was influenced by its colonial ruler, Britain. Anwar Sadat grew up wanting Egypt to become independent from European influence.

Anwar Sadat felt that the events of his life closely followed events that were important to Egypt. From a very early age, he felt that his life and Egypt's fate were intertwined. He wrote in the prologue to his autobiography, "[T]he story of my life is at the same time the story of Egypt since 1918, for so destiny has decreed. The events of my life have coincided with those which Egypt has lived during that period."

Humble Beginnings

Anwar Sadat was born on December 25, 1918, in Mit Abul Kum, Egypt. Sadat was one of thirteen children and grew up in the small farming village beside the Nile River. Sadat's father, Mohammed el-Sadat, was a clerk in a military hospital. He had completed enough schooling to earn his General Certificate of Primary Education. Today, we think of education as a basic need for all people. This was not so in Egypt before the twentieth century. Mohammed el-Sadat's elementary school education was unusual for Egyptian villagers at that time. Many villagers could not even read or write. In fact, the highest hope that a villager could have was to become the sheikh. A sheikh is the head of a mosque, where Muslims go to worship. Despite such a humble education, Sadat's father was called the *effendi*, or professor.

Anwar Sadat had a close relationship with his grandmother. She lived with his family in Mit Abul Kum. Young Anwar liked to run errands for her. He did such things as bring jars of treacle (molasses) from the ship when it arrived to deliver goods to the river town. The young boy delighted in the simple village life. He loved working the land with his neighbors.

Egypt has a hot, dry climate, and water is scarce. In order for the villagers to farm the land, they had to irrigate it, or gather and distribute water to moisten the land. All the villagers pitched in to help irrigate everyone's

Focus on Egypt

Egypt is on the northeastern tip of the African continent and contains the Nile River, which empties into the Mediterranean Sea. Egypt is more than 386,000 square miles (1,000,000 sq. km) in area. This is about the size of France and Spain put together. The Nile River runs through the center of Egypt. Most of Egypt's land is desert. The Nile River valley and delta are the places where there is enough water for farmers to grow crops. Therefore, most of Egypt's population lives in these areas. Put together, these fertile lands are about as big as the country of Denmark. That is not such a big area for about 43 million people to live! The people who live in the desert are nomads. Nomads have no fixed home. They travel with their animals, searching for land on which the animals can graze.

Egypt is one of the most populous countries in Africa. Its size is equal to a large portion of the eastern United States (upper left inset).

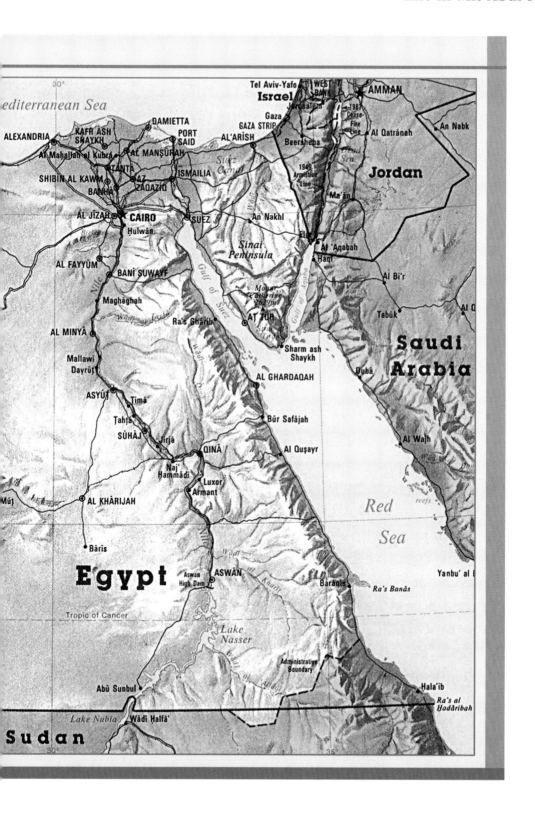

land. No one worked simply for himself. The whole village helped to irrigate each farm one by one. As a young boy, Sadat loved this sense of community. He liked that people felt good about working together for a common goal instead of simply working for themselves. In his autobiography, he wrote, "That kind of collective work—with and for other men, with no profit or any kind of individual reward in prospect—made me feel that I belonged not merely to my immediate family at home, or even to the big family of the village, but to something vaster and more significant: the land." It was this feeling that would kindle in the young boy a desire to free his beloved Egypt from Britain's rule.

How Egypt Became Part of the British Empire

When Sadat was growing up, Egypt was a colony in the British Empire. It had taken the better part of a century for Egypt to fall under British control. In the nineteenth century, Egypt became part of the Ottoman Empire (its central government was present-day Turkey). Then in 1805, Muhammad Ali, a Turkish army officer, overthrew the Ottoman governor in Egypt. Ali declared himself the ruler of Egypt. Ali was the person who built the first Suez Canal. The canal linked the Mediterranean Sea to the Red Sea at the Gulf of Suez. The Suez Canal was an important trade route. France helped Ali to accomplish his task. Britain, France's longtime enemy, took notice of the project. In 1875, Britain bought a share in the canal. Buying a share in a project meant paying money for its upkeep in return for some of the project's profits. Egypt's leader agreed to the sale because the country desperately needed money at the time. It was just the

■ Work on the modern Suez Canal was done mostly by hand. Shown here is an 1860s photograph of men digging through the clay to form a trench near the Red Sea end of the canal.

event Britain needed to get its foot in Egypt's door. After the sale, Britain and France divided up the control of Egypt between them. They didn't exactly call Egypt a colony. They called Egypt the Veiled Protectorate because Britain really called all the shots in Egypt, while only pretending to be offering help and money to Egypt. Later, in 1919, the nationalist Wafd Party was formed in Egypt. The party led an uprising against the British, which failed. However, more and more people joined the movement for independence. These people would eventually help Sadat and other soldiers overthrow British rule in Egypt.

Firing a Small Boy's Imagination

Sadat's grandmother told him bedtime stories every night. These stories fueled his imagination for a glorious new Egypt. These stories were not fairy tales but real stories of heroic men who did brave things for their countries. Some of these people were Egyptian martyrs who had died for their country. Every night, Sadat's grandmother told him the story of Zahran, the hero of Denshway. Denshway was a village that was 3 miles (4.8 kilometers) away from Mit Abul Kum. As the story went, British soldiers in Denshway were shooting pigeons and accidentally set a wheat silo on fire. Farmers gathered and the British soldiers shot at them. The farmers began to fight back. In the struggle, a British soldier died. Many people were arrested and were brought before a judge. Some of the farmers were whipped. Others were sentenced to be hanged. Zahran was the first to be hanged. According to the story, Zahran held his head high on his way to his death. Sadat's grandmother told him that Zahran was a man of great courage, even to his death. Sadat felt proud that Zahran had stood up to the British and had helped to kill one of them.

Sadat realized as a small boy that something was wrong in Egypt. This was long before he ever saw any British officers. He felt Egypt should not have British soldiers causing trouble in peaceful villages such as Denshway. He learned to hate the British, who whipped Egyptian farmers and hanged Egyptian citizens.

The History of Egypt

The Macedonian king Alexander the Great (356–323 BC) crosses the Euphrates River with his army to fight Darius III of Persia.

For 3,000 years, Egypt was ruled by dynasties of pharaohs, or kings. Persians invaded and conquered Egypt in the sixth century BC. Alexander the Great of Macedonia kicked the Persians out of Egypt in 332 BC. Alexander the Great, upon his death, granted control of Egypt to a Greek general, Ptolemy. The Greeks ruled Egypt for the next 300 years. The Romans took over Egypt when Queen Cleopatra, who was part of the royal family of the Ptolemies, died in the first century BC. The Roman Empire split into eastern and western halves in AD 395. Rome was invaded by the Visigoths in 410, and by 476, Germans ruled the western half. The eastern half continued as the Byzantine Empire, and Egypt was part of that until AD 642, when Muslim Arabs conquered Egypt.

Going to School and Playing in the Village

The job of a military clerk did not pay much money. There were thirteen children to feed in the Sadat family. This required every family member to do his or her part to keep the family going. Sadat, like many other village children, helped with farmwork. He looked forward to each of the seasonal tasks of farm life: irrigating time, planting seeds, and harvesting the wheat when it had grown strong in the rich Nile soil.

Like many village children, Sadat had his small allowance with which he could buy a cup of tea for refreshment during his lunch break at school. His grandmother insisted that he go to school. He attended the Koranic Teaching School in Mit Abul Kum. There he learned to read and write. He also learned by heart the teachings of the Koran, the Muslim holy book. Nonetheless, Sadat's teachers complained that he was better at daydreaming than at his lessons. What was he thinking about all the time, with his mind so far away? He was thinking about doing great things for Egypt and about Kemal Atatürk, Mohandas Gandhi,

■ Kemal Atatürk, future president of Turkey, talks with his advisers during a winter campaign in 1919. While a student, Sadat read about Atatürk's military successes against the Ottoman Empire. Sadat saw in Atatürk a role model who worked to free his people.

and Adolf Hitler. At first glance, it might not be easy to see what each of these men has in common. Sadat idolized each of these men because each of them, in his own way, had stood up to an oppressive power and fought for what he thought was right.

Kemal Atatürk was a man who had overthrown the Ottoman Empire, which had ruled for centuries in Turkey. Atatürk became Turkey's first president in 1923. In Atatürk, Sadat had a powerful example of a man who had freed his country from the rule of detached kings. Mohandas Gandhi was another important figure for the young boy. Gandhi was the leader of a movement for Indian independence. He helped to overthrow British rule in India. Gandhi toured Egypt in 1932 to speak about his policy of peaceful revolution. Sadat greatly admired Gandhi and strove to imitate him. He dressed in a white apron so that he could look like Gandhi, who wore a simple white robe. Sadat would often sit atop his house wearing his white apron, pretending to be like Gandhi. Sadat's father would have to tell him he should come down because he would catch pneumonia from sitting outside in the winter wearing nothing but an apron!

Later, Sadat also looked up to Adolf Hitler, the leader of Nazi Germany in the 1930s and 1940s. Sadat admired Hitler, not for his warring or his hatred, but because Hitler had created a Germany that could hold its own against Britain. At the time, there were not many nations that could stand up to British power. Sadat hated Britain so much that it seemed natural for him to admire any nation that could be powerful and independent from Britain. However, Sadat did not know about the many horrible things Hitler did in Germany. He would learn

■ Sadat admired Nazi leader Adolf Hitler for standing up to the British. In Sadat's worldview, a free Egypt was paramount to anything else in life. Overthrowing the British was the first step.

about those, like so many people in the world, after the end of World War II (1939–1945).

Sadat's Education

The Sadat family moved closer to Cairo in 1925. The family lived in a small house in Kubri Al-Qubba, near Cairo. Sadat went to a private school called the Islamic Benevolent Society School. Sadat walked to and from school every day. On his way, he passed Al-Qubba Palace. He and his friends sometimes stole apricots from the palace grounds. This was a brave and foolhardy thing to do because touching anything of the king's could literally get you killed in Egypt. Sadat had no idea at the time that he would one day sit on the very chair on which King Fuad and then King Farouk sat.

In 1930, Sadat earned his General Certificate of Primary Education at the Sultan Hussein School in Cairo. Afterward, he and his older brother joined the Fuad I Secondary School (equal to a high school). The Sadat family could barely afford the fees to send both boys to school, so it is fortunate that Sadat's brother quickly decided to drop out of school.

Sadat's high school education was not a smooth process, but he did complete it. Students in Egypt at that time had to fill out paperwork to qualify for examinations. If they passed the examinations, they received certificates. Sadat passed the examination for the General Certificate of Secondary Education but didn't do well enough to qualify in the grade for the next certificate, the General Certificate of Proficiency (GCP). Showing his spirit of independence, Sadat took his papers and enrolled at another school, where he earned his

■ Cairo in the 1930s was already a huge, crowded city. Sadat attended high school in Cairo. Soon after, Sadat saw in its people an Egyptian nationalism that could be fueled to force an overthrow of the weak Egyptian king.

GCP. Then he enrolled at his old school for the next stage in his education, which he passed, again not well enough to qualify him for the final stage. Again, Sadat took his papers elsewhere to complete his final year. He passed in individual subjects, but his general marks were unsatisfactory. Once again and for the last time, he had to go to another school to get his final certificate, the General Certificate of Education. While there, Sadat joined other students in anti-British demonstrations. After gaining his high school certificate, the next step was the military academy.

CHAPTER TWO

REVOLUTIONARY YOUTH

■ Egyptian military cadets train with rifles and bayonets. Sadat saw military life as an important step in coming of age. He would use the military system to help Egypt expel British soldiers from the country.

In 1936, Sadat earned a chance to educate himself further by attending the military academy. Britain had agreed to help establish the military academy in Egypt as part of a plan to help Egypt add to and support its armies and its military defense system.

Sadat wrote in his autobiography, "the British helped me to join the military academy when the reason why I wanted to join in the first place was to kick them out of Egypt."

Applying to the Royal Military Academy

The Royal Military Academy in Egypt permitted members of the Egyptian middle class to attend. It even provided spaces for those students whose family income was lower than average. However, there were two requirements that were not so easy to meet. First, an applicant had to give details of his father's property and income. Second, he had to have a reference. It couldn't be any old reference either. It needed to be from someone who was highly placed in the government. The process was similar to applying to a military academy in the United States, for which a government official must offer a recommendation. Sadat's father worked as a military clerk, so the first requirement would be met. The second requirement took a bit of doing. Sadat's father used his connections in the military to get young Sadat an audience of sorts with the chairman of the committee that looked at the application forms.

■ The Royal Military Academy trained its officers to be excellent
horsemen. Sadat's military education also included studying
great historical battles. Outside of class, Sadat read books on
Egypt's social history.

Sadat and his father stood in the hallway of the chairman's house, waiting for him to pass by them. Their plan was simple: When the chairman passed, they would explain to him that they needed him to recommend young Sadat to the academy. Amazingly, the plan went off without a hitch. The chairman was too busy to listen for long and merely said, "What? Yes, all right," and that was that. Sadat was all set to enroll. His name was on the list, although because his reference was the least impressive reference (some people listed the crown prince Muhammad Ali as a reference), Sadat was on the bottom of the enrollment list.

Then Sadat ran into a bit of bad luck.

The war minister, Hamdi Saif al-Nasr, decided that he wanted six places at the military academy to be reserved for his relatives. The last six students whose names were on the enrollment list would not get to attend the academy. Sadat's hopes were dashed at first. He was disappointed and wondered what he would do if he could not attend the academy. By a stroke of good luck and timing, various people spoke on his behalf. Suddenly, the academy accepted him. He began classes twenty-six days after the other students had started. He was a little late but ready for the task ahead.

Education at the Academy

At the academy, students learned traditional subjects such as math and science. They also studied Egyptian history and the strategy of famous military battles. Sadat continued to revere Atatürk while studying at the academy. Apart from his regular studies, he read books about Turkish history and the Turkish revolution. He also studied in detail

■ Mahatma Gandhi showed the world that the British could be defeated using peaceful means. Sadat admired Gandhi's leadership but did not think much of peaceful uprising. He was a military man and saw armed conflict as the best and quickest way to change Egypt's future.

the events that had led to the British occupation of Egypt. Sadat could hardly wait to graduate and to begin to do something for Egypt.

Sadat graduated from the academy in 1938. He began his military training and also married the woman whom his parents had picked out for him. He was twenty years old and an officer in Egypt's armed forces, yet his mind was firmly on revolution. Although he had long admired Gandhi, he did not seek to imitate his peaceful ways, as he had played at doing when he was a boy. Sadat was convinced that only forceful means would work to liberate Egypt from British colonialism. Part of this decision came from knowing about the Egyptian government. It was weak, and its officials did whatever the British wanted them to do. Sadat believed that only through armed revolution could the country be ripped from both strangling governments.

First Duties and Secret Plans

Sadat was stationed in Manqabad, a small town in upper Egypt. He held meetings in his room and in the officers' mess tent. His mission was to educate his fellow officers about the political situation in Egypt. He did not suggest any solutions to the problem because he wanted the officers to work together in figuring out solutions. Sadat wanted to educate himself culturally as well. He thought that having a firm basis in cultural arts would help him in politics. He ordered books from Cairo and sat in cafés on his rare evenings off, reading when his friends went drinking. He even applied to the British Institute, to try to get a B.A. from the University of London, but he did not get in. He concentrated his

■ Sadat frequented tea houses like the café shown here during his military service. He was not there to socialize, however. Sadat used his free time to study. He liked to read history and politics.

Gamal Abdel Nasser

Gamal Abdel Nasser was born in Alexandria in 1918. His father was a postman. Young Nasser had humble origins but big dreams. He was educated in Cairo, at the Royal Military Academy, as Sadat was. After graduating from the academy, he became a soldier, and while he was in the army, he met others who shared his dream of a new government for Egypt. Nasser and these soldiers, including Anwar Sadat, founded the Free Officers Organization. The group would overthrow King Farouk in 1952, and Nasser would rule Egypt as president from 1952 until his death from a heart attack in 1970. One of Nasser's first acts as ruler was to negotiate the end of Britain's seventy-two-year rule of Egypt. Nasser's achievements as president of Egypt included the nationalization of the Suez Canal in 1956 and the building of the Aswan High Dam on the Nile River in 1968. Nasser was also president of the United Arab Republic, which united Syria and Egypt, from 1958 to 1961. Nasser also wrote a book, *The Revolution's Philosophy*.

Egyptian president Gamal Abdel Nasser attends the inauguration of an oil refinery near Cairo.

energy on Egypt's political situation with his fellow officers in meetings. It was during one of these meetings that he met Gamal Abdel Nasser for the first time.

In 1939, Sadat and Nasser formed a revolutionary group called the Free Officers Organization. These young men knew that the political hot spot for Egypt was in Cairo, the nation's capital. They could do relatively little in the way of political action when they were stationed at the small outpost of Manqabad. Then Sadat and a few of his fellow officers got a lucky break. They were chosen to take a course at the Signals School of Maadi, near Cairo, in 1939.

Nasser joined the group in Cairo six months later. There, the young officers continued their meetings. Sadat decided that he wanted a permanent position in the Signal Corps. At the graduation ceremony from the Signals School course, he gave a speech that he recited from memory instead of reading from a paper. It impressed the Signal Corps so much that Sadat was asked to join. He would be stationed in Maadi, near Cairo, and would not have to go back to a distant little town. His revolutionary activities could finally go into high gear. It was one of the happiest moments of his life.

Secret Work for the German Military

Hitler won several victories against the British between 1939 and 1941 during World War II. Sadat saw his chance to speed up the process of revolution while the British were occupied in dealing with Germany. His plan was an armed revolution to overthrow British rule in Egypt.

In the summer of 1942, German forces under the command of General Erwin Rommel reached the

■ Sadat *(right)* sits next to Major Kamal Al-Din Hussein, a fellow member of the Free Officers Organization. Hussein would become chief of Egypt's new National Liberation Army. This army was composed of volunteers from the National Guard, Youth Legion, and other home defense forces. Women were included in this defense force.

Egyptian fort at Alamein, near Alexandria. In the streets of Cairo, crowds gathered to welcome the Germans. Sadat and the Free Officers tried to get a message to Rommel, saying that they would like to work with him. However, the message did not make it to Rommel. Sadat then tried to deliver an Egyptian general who had been dismissed by the British into German hands.

The British learned of this move and arrested Sadat. He was sent to jail. Sadat served his prison sentence in light detention. This meant that he had supervised outings and did not always have to remain inside the prison. After serving two years of his sentence, Sadat escaped during one of the supervised outings. He was now a fugitive from British justice.

Sadat spent the next few months working whatever small jobs he could find in order to earn money to send to his family. He grew a beard and worked under the assumed name Hadji Muhammd. The end of World War II in 1945 saw the end of martial (military) law in Egypt. Sadat could stop living and working as a fugitive and return to his normal life. He had been a fugitive for three years.

The Free Officers Attack

Nasser headed the Free Officers Organization while Sadat was imprisoned and on the run. When Sadat reunited with his revolutionary friends, his first thought was to plan a terrorist act. He suggested blowing up the British Embassy. Nasser thought this was a bad idea. Sadat then suggested killing an Egyptian official named Amin Osman Pasha. Osman Pasha worked for the British and cooperated with their rule of the Egyptian people.

■ Sadat spent time in a prison cell much like the one shown here. The part he played in the assassination of Osman Pasha proved Sadat was ready to do what he thought necessary to carry Egypt to freedom.

Israel

Palestine has long been a land that many different groups wanted to claim. The Hebrews settled in the area around 2,000 BC and controlled the area in the twelfth century BC. They ruled it until the Romans invaded in 63 BC. The Jews rebelled against the Romans many times. Each time they rebelled, the Romans took the rebels and moved them somewhere else, for instance, to Alexandria, Egypt. The Jews spread across the world in what is known as the Diaspora, which means "scattering" in Greek.

During the late nineteenth century, a movement known as Zionism gained popularity. Zionist Jews wanted to return to Palestine. In 1917, British foreign secretary Sir Arthur Balfour met with Jewish leaders and then announced the Balfour Declaration. The declaration stated that Britain would work for "the establishment in Palestine of a national home for the Jewish people." This nation would finally be formed in 1948 and would be called Israel.

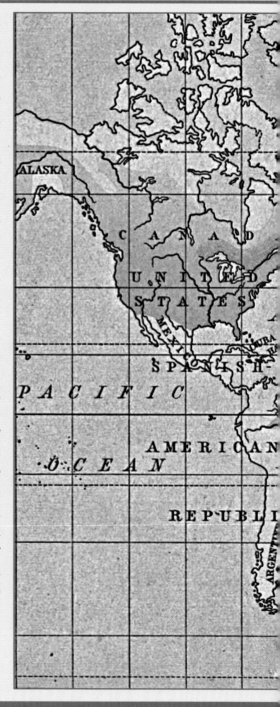

The ancient Jewish Diaspora scattered families around the world.

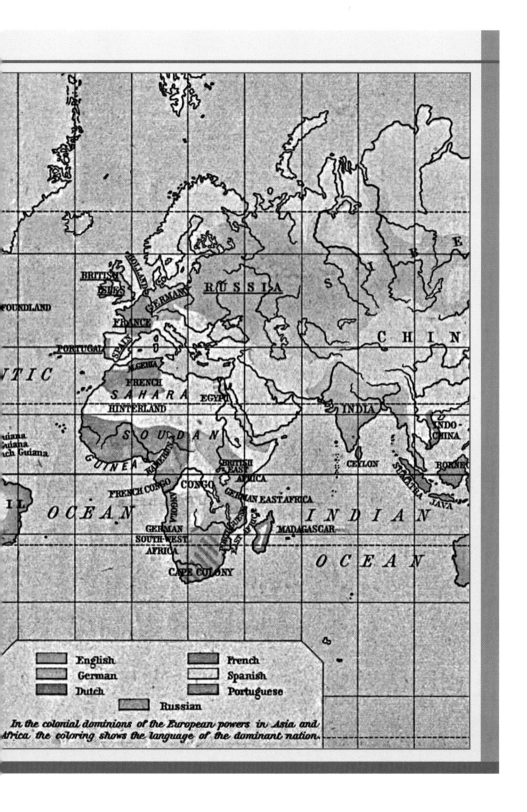

English
German
Dutch
Russian

French
Spanish
Portuguese

In the colonial dominions of the European powers in Asia and
Africa the coloring shows the language of the dominant nation.

The Free Officers planned the assassination and carried it out. Sadat and his friends considered Osman Pasha's assassination a victory for their cause. This damaged the idea of British protection in Egypt. The British learned of Sadat's involvement and arrested him. He received a sentence of two years in prison.

Changing His Life

At first, Sadat was put in solitary confinement, in a small dark cell. He was not even allowed to read. When he was transferred to another cell and given reading privileges, he taught himself French and English. He also began to keep a diary. Sadat had plenty of time to reflect on his life, and he wrote down his feelings about his life, the military, the British, and Egypt. He decided that if he was going to overthrow a tradition of oppression in Egypt, he had to start by overthrowing a few traditions of his own. He decided to divorce his wife, whom he had married because his parents had arranged the marriage.

Other events conspired to show Sadat how his destiny and the destiny of Egypt were bound intimately with those of other Arab nations. War had broken out between Israel and neighboring Arab countries on May 15, 1948. The newly formed United Nations decided that Palestine should be divided into two separate states, one for Arabs and one for Jews. The Arab nations hated the idea of Palestine's partition. On the day Israel became an official country, Egypt, Iraq, Lebanon, Syria, and Transjordan (present-day Jordan) attacked Israel. Gamal Abdel Nasser was wounded in this attack. It was then that Nasser realized how insep-arable Egypt's fate was from those of other Arab

■ Sadat embraced civilian life after his time spent in jail. Having a normal life as a businessman at first appealed to Sadat. This way of life soon wore thin with him, though. As a civilian, Sadat knew he could never make social changes that would help free Egypt from corrupt or foreign rulers.

J ehan Sadat

Jehan Sadat, second wife of Egyptian president Anwar Sadat, worked for women's rights in Egypt while married to Sadat. Today, she continues to work for women's rights in the world. Jehan was instrumental in the Egyptian Civil Rights Law that gave more rights to women in Egypt. Jehan was active in the cause long before she met Anwar Sadat. She started a women's emancipation group in her village, Talla. The group aimed to help women become less dependent on their husbands and more self-sufficient. Jehan believes that one way women can do this is through education. She helps to promote literacy throughout the world.

Jehan Sadat sits for an interview in 1987.

nations, and he took pains to convince his fellow Free Officers of this fact.

However, when Sadat left prison for the second time, he did not enlist in the armed forces. He decided to see what life as a civilian was like. The first thing he did was buy some nice clothes and go to a health spa. Sadat was always concerned with his appearance and his health.

Civilian Life

Sadat decided that he wanted to try being an actor. He took out an ad in a Cairo magazine in which he gave his age, height, acting interests, and desires for comic acting in theater or film. His ad was unsuccessful, however.

Sadat had much more success in the business world. Shortly after his release from prison, Sadat met up with a former friend, Hassan Izzat. Izzat invited Sadat to his house in Suez. There, Sadat helped Izzat conduct some business in publishing, for which he was handsomely paid. In fact, he was paid so well that he decided to go back to the health spa for a while. Before he could do this, however, he met a woman named Jehan. She was Izzat's wife's cousin. Sadat was smitten with Jehan, and they soon began to date.

The publishing work Sadat did during this time turned out to be profitable for him. A publishing company published Sadat's prison diary. The company also offered Sadat a job as an editor. He worked in publishing until December 1948, when he went into business in Suez with Hassan Izzat. Shortly thereafter, he proposed to Jehan. They were married in early 1949. Sadat and his new wife moved to Zaqziq on May 29, 1949. Sadat's business ventures lasted for only six months before he decided to return to the army. It took a little string pulling, but in January 1950, Sadat was reinstated into the army at the rank of captain. This was the same rank he had held when he left the army. Many of his colleagues, however, had already been promoted twice, to major and then to lieutenant colonel.

CHAPTER THREE

A CHANGING EGYPT AND MIDDLE EAST

■ A parade in Cairo in 1951 commemorates Egyptians who were killed by British troops during recent anti-British riots. The banners call for boycott of British goods in the city. Egyptian nationalism was paving the way for the Free Officers's coup.

Gamal Abdel Nasser was one of the first people to call on Sadat to congratulate him on his reinstatement in the army. Nasser told Sadat that the Free Officers Organization had gotten quite powerful and could help Sadat with his army promotions. The higher Sadat's rank in the army, the more he could help the Free Officers Organization.

Sadat took his promotion tests and was promoted to lieutenant colonel in 1951. Nasser suggested that Sadat keep a low profile because he would be watched owing to his past record of political activity. Still, Nasser gave Sadat a list of the Free Officers in the army. Sadat set about getting to know them. They never talked of politics for fear that they would blow their cover. They only got together to socialize.

Nasser Asserts His Leadership

Nasser ran the Free Officers Organization differently than Sadat had. Nasser created secret cells, or groups of officers. There was an atmosphere of secrecy within the organization. No one knew who belonged to it, except for members of one's own cell. The organization was planning to overthrow King Farouk. Nasser felt that secrecy was the key to success.

In January 1952, British troops attacked a rebel Egyptian police force in Ismailia. This led to rioting in Cairo. People were fed up with King Farouk. The Free Officers knew that it would soon be time to overthrow their king. In fact, the riot in 1952 convinced Nasser to hasten the time for the coup. On July 22, Sadat returned home from the movies to discover a message from Nasser. The message directed him to join his fellow officers in Cairo right away. It would be Sadat's job, as public relations minister, to announce the coup on the radio.

The announcement was broadcast on July 23 at 7:00 AM. In his autobiography, Sadat described how the streets looked to him when he came out of the radio station after announcing the coup: "I saw the streets of the metropolis crowded with people as I had never seen them before. Old and young, women and children, were kissing each other, shaking hands, coming together in small clusters or large circles—but all the time in total silence." Sadat's next task would be to supervise the abdication of King Farouk, on July 26. Sadat flew to Alexandria to accomplish the job.

The question in the minds of the Free Officers and the rest of Egypt was, What would Nasser do now? The Free Officers wanted him to take control of Egypt in a dictatorship. The first thing Nasser did was to name the new group in power the Revolutionary Command Council. This group, with Nasser at its head, would rule Egypt from 1952 until Nasser's death in 1970. Sadat was first made a minister of state in this government. Eventually Sadat rose in rank and became Nasser's vice president. One of the tasks Sadat performed as minister of state was to create a newspaper, called *Al-Gumhuriah*. He headed the newspaper as editor in chief.

The End of British Rule

The elections of 1952 unanimously elected Nasser as chairman of the Revolutionary Command Council. After a struggle among the officers of the Revolutionary Command Council, Nasser became the indisputable leader. In 1954, Britain signed the evacuation agreement, and the British left Egypt. The last British officer would be gone from Egypt by June 19, 1956.

The new government became a role model for countries that wanted to stay free of an alignment with the

■ Colonel Anwar Sadat enjoys a light moment following the successful military overthrow of Egypt's King Farouk. The Free Officers had finally freed the Egyptian people from bad governance by a corrupt ruler.

superpowers of Russia and the United States. During 1953, Egypt tried to negotiate a deal for weapons with both the United States and the Soviet Union. The deals did not go through because both of the superpowers wanted too much from Egypt in terms of loyalty. For instance, the United States agreed to give Egypt weapons only if Egypt would agree never to attack the United States or U.S. allies. Egypt refused, saying that such a deal would compromise Egypt's liberty, which had been earned so slowly and with such hard work.

The Suez Canal Crisis

In 1956, a project was in the works that would have the world watching breathlessly as Egypt tried to cooperate with the superpowers. This project was the Aswan High Dam. Several Western nations, such as Britain and France, agreed to help finance the building of the Aswan High Dam. Nasser accepted the proposal. During the construction of the dam, Egypt did negotiate an arms deal with Russia. The United States was not so happy about this. Russia was a Communist country, and its political system was seen as the enemy of democracy. Around the same time, Egypt also recognized China, which was another Communist country. The United States got so angry that it talked its allies, who were financing the dam project, into withholding the money needed to complete the dam.

In response, Nasser nationalized the Suez Canal. Egypt suddenly took possession of the canal, ending French and English control of its operation and profits. The canal and the surrounding lands became Egyptian property. In his book *In Search of Identity*, Sadat wrote that he felt proud listening to Nasser's radio speech describing the Suez Canal nationalization. Sadat loved the fact that Egypt could speak loud and clear as an independent country, even against some of the most powerful nations in the world. Britain and France had been sharing the money made from the Suez Canal shortcut between sea routes of Europe to Asia. This had been an important trade route since the nineteenth century. What would Nasser do with the money coming to Egypt from the Suez Canal? He used it to build the Aswan Dam.

In October 1956, the British and the French responded to Nasser's bold move. They helped the Israelis capture the Gaza Strip and the Sinai Peninsula from Egypt. Nasser's response was to contact the United States and ask President Dwight Eisenhower to persuade Britain and France—both U.S. allies—to stay out of Arab affairs. Nasser felt that Egypt could deal with Israel if Egypt and Israel were left to fight the battle themselves, without the interference of the West. The Israelis withdrew in March 1957. This made Nasser more popular than ever in Egypt and in the eyes of Arabs everywhere.

Shortly afterward, in 1958, Egypt and Syria declared unity between them and created the United Arab Republic (UAR). Nasser was named president of the republic. Most Arab countries feared the UAR. Saudi Arabia, in particular, was not happy. Saudi Arabia shared a border with Syria and wanted Syria to remain neutral. The Egyptian-Syrian alliance disturbed the balance of power in the Middle East.

Sadat happened to be good friends with King Faisal of Saudi Arabia. Faisal had dinner with Sadat when the king was on a tour of Egypt, shortly after the UAR had

■ The Suez Canal connects the Mediterranean Sea with the Red Sea (which feeds into the Indian Ocean). The Great Bitter Lake represents the middle of the canal. The Nile River delta is on the left. To the right is the Sinai Peninsula.

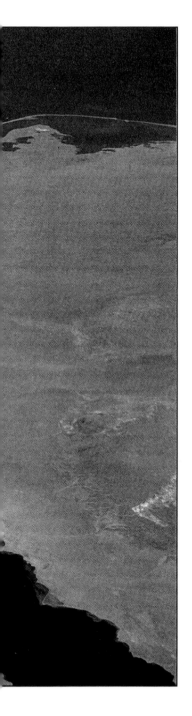

been set up. Faisal warned Sadat that the alliance would end badly for Egypt. Syria, he said, was not to be trusted. In fact, Syria withdrew from the UAR in 1962.

Changes Inside Egypt

What was going on inside Egypt during Nasser's presidency? The government had started out democratically. It had a real interest in benefiting the everyday lives of the Egyptian people. The people needed more freedoms than they had under King Farouk and British rule. They also did not have the benefits of social services that all great nations provide their people. Therefore, health care and education improved dramatically under the new Egyptian government.

In addition, Nasser changed the rules of land ownership in Egypt. He limited the amount of land that one person could own. This gave farmers who owned small pieces of land more of a chance to increase the size of their farms. That was not the only change in Egypt's landscape. The rise of industrialization saw high-rise buildings in Cairo constructed near mosques that had been in the city since the tenth century. Nasser promoted some

■ As a colonel before the Suez Crisis, Sadat often met with British military leaders still controlling the zone. Here he stands with General Sir Charles Keightley outside Keightley's offices. Sadat gained valuable experience during these times, which would help him become the honored president of Egypt later in life.

wonderful changes for the Egyptian people, and on the average, income increased.

However, population growth continued to increase, while available farmland decreased. By the end of Nasser's career, there were fewer peasants who owned land than there had been at the beginning of his presidency. Part of the reason for this was the Committee of the Liquidation of Feudalism, which was supposed to modernize farming methods in Egypt. What the committee also did was seize land from the people for government use.

Sadat was shocked when he visited his home village of Mit Abul Kum. On that visit, Sadat found that in the nearby village of Talla, mayors and citizens had lost their jobs. Worse, their property had been seized by the state. Sadat knew these people, having grown up with them. He knew that these people had supported the revolution. They supported progress in Egypt. It was not fair that their property was seized. Sadat drove back to Cairo and located the official responsible for this, demanding that he reverse the decision, which he did.

To add to the confusion, there was fighting among members of the military, as military leaders could not agree on Egyptian policies. Although Nasser started by embracing democratic ideals, in practice he was actually running Egypt like a dictatorship. The unrest Egypt experienced in the 1960s peaked in 1967 during a war with Israel called the Six-Day War.

The Six-Day War

In May 1967, Nasser was told by the Soviets that Israel was going to attack Syria. This information was wrong,

■ Nasser meets with Cuban leader Fidel Castro outside the Hotel Theresa in New York City in 1960. Nasser's attempts to pull Egypt out of financial ruin forced him to ally himself with other countries. He did not want to do business with either the United States or the Soviet Union.

but Nasser believed the Soviet warning. Nasser ordered Egyptian troops to go to the Sinai Peninsula and to cut off access to the southern Israeli port of Eilat. He asked the United Nations to remove the troops it had stationed in the border area. The UN did so quickly. The Egyptian troops then took positions near the Israeli border. On June 5, 1967, Israel took its first step to claiming the Sinai Peninsula. Israeli aircraft attacked the Egyptian air force and nearly wiped it out. Egypt was in a poor position to fight back, as 309 of its 340 aircraft had been destroyed. Israeli ground forces captured the Sinai Peninsula. The forces marched to within ten miles (16 km) of the Suez Canal in just three days. This was a stunning victory that left Egypt reeling. Egypt suffered heavy losses. Around 3,000 Egyptian soldiers died. Syria and Jordan also joined the war. Their armies proved no match against Israel's. This allowed Israel to conquer the Golan Heights and the western bank of the Jordan River.

The Israeli victory in the Six-Day War took such a toll on Nasser's health that his close associates were unsure whether he would live through

Origins of the Six-Day War

The tensions that resulted in the Six-Day War in 1967 were a long time brewing. When Israel was created as a country in 1948, it shocked the Islamic Arab world surrounding the tiny country. Israel fought with Egypt over the Sinai lands in 1956 and won. Egyptians always found it hard to live down the disgrace of being beaten by the newer, smaller country. They planned to get their revenge on Israel. Although the United Nations eventually sent troops into the Sinai to keep the peace, Egyptian president Nasser became more determined to regain the land. He ordered the troops out of the Sinai during the spring of 1967, and when the troops left, they left the area open for warfare. Nasser ordered Egyptian troops to block off Israel's southern access to the Red Sea, which was a clear act of war. The Six-Day War involved three nations against Israel: Egypt, Jordan, and Syria. Against the odds, Israel managed to gain territory and rout the entire Egyptian air force in the bargain. That happened early in the Six-Day War, on June 5, and with no air force, Egypt's foot soldiers did not have much success. By June 7, the Israelis were in control of the Gaza Strip and the Suez Canal. Israel sent paratroopers to gain back Israel's access to the Red Sea. On June 8, Nasser accepted a cease-fire, an offer to stop fighting. It was humiliating not only for Egypt, but also for the country that had given Egypt so many weapons and military support: the Soviet Union.

An Egyptian tank lies destroyed by the side of a road after an Israeli attack during the Six-Day War.

■ Sadat knew the importance of keeping close relations with Arab leaders across the Middle East. Here he embraces Palestinian leader Yasser Arafat after taking control of Egypt following Nasser's death.

it. He did live through the crisis, but he was so upset at Egypt's losses that he resigned his post. People gathered in the street, shouting for his return to the presidency. With such a show of support, Nasser returned to his position. When he did so, he had to think about rebuilding Egypt after its losses.

Some Arab governments, such as Saudi Arabia, lent Nasser the money to rebuild Egypt's defenses. In return, Nasser agreed to stop attacking them in his speeches. Then he worked on how to rebuild the military. The Soviet Union sent technicians to Nasser's aid. The 1950s had seen great promise in Egypt after Nasser came to power. Much of the 1960s saw conflict in Egypt alongside the progress.

CHAPTER FOUR

PRESIDENT SADAT

■ The Egyptian Revolutionary Council poses for a photo in Cairo. These men brought Egypt into the modern world. Sadat *(standing, second from left)* had a close friendship with Nasser. This friendship and his administrative competence helped him rise to vice president in 1969.

In 1969, Nasser made Anwar Sadat vice president of Egypt. Nasser never really recovered his health after Egypt's losses during the Six-Day War. He was always ill after that. His diabetes worsened, and he was in and out of the hospital. In 1969, Nasser had a heart attack.

Shortly afterward, two events happened that caused uproar in the Arab world. In September 1970, the conflict in nearby Jordan unsettled Egypt and much of the Arab world. There was a Palestinian Arab nationalist movement in Jordan started by the Palestine Liberation Organization (PLO). King Hussein of Jordan felt threatened by this organization, and the army attacked the PLO. The PLO was driven out of Jordan. Before this event, much of the Arab world believed that Palestinian rights would be gained by victory over Israel. Nasser always publicly supported the Palestinians' right to their homeland.

However, Nasser's growing opinion was that Egypt should make peace with Israel. Egypt was a leader in the Arab world, and if fighting happened with Israel, Egypt would have much to lose. That was one reason why Nasser was interested in keeping the peace. At the same time, he wanted to preserve unity in the Arab world. With this interest in mind, Nasser held a conference in 1970 called the Arab Summit Conference. All of the heads of state in the Arab world were there, even King Hussein of Jordan. The conference was such hard work that Nasser's health, already delicate, gave out immediately after. Nasser escorted all the Arab heads of state to the airport after the conference. He collapsed that afternoon and was dead by evening.

Sadat's Election to the Presidency

Before Nasser died, Sadat thought it would be a good idea for him to remain vice president until Egypt had recovered from the losses it sustained in the Six-Day War. Nasser had declared, in his speech on reassuming the presidency in 1967, that presidential elections should only be held after Egypt had recovered from those losses. However, after Nasser died, Sadat decided it was time to step up and help his country recover. He wanted to do this as the president of Egypt. He decided to run for president.

One reason Sadat ran for president was that there was a Socialist Soviet-influenced group in the Egyptian government that wanted to take power. Sadat did not want all the hard work he and Nasser had done to be for nothing. He did not want Communists to come in and rule people as the British or the king had. Sadat wanted to work for the people and create a stronger, more prosperous Egypt.

Sadat had two other reasons to run for the presidency. The first was that the president of Algeria came to Cairo to urge Sadat to take the presidency. It was important, President Houari Boumedienne said, for Egypt not to lose respect in the eyes of the world. Egypt needed a strong leader

■ Arab leaders from around the Middle East attend Gamal Abdel Nasser's funeral. Sadat *(far left)* chose to run for the presidency to rebuild Egypt after the devastating 1967 war.

in order to appear as a strong nation to the rest of the world. Sadat, of course, agreed with the Algerian president. Finally, the last reason he decided to run was that the leaders of the armed forces wrote a letter to Sadat, urging him to lead the country in these trying times. They asked Sadat to be their supreme commander while they helped to rebuild Egypt.

On October 15, 1970, Sadat was elected as the president of Egypt.

Gaining Leadership Credibility

At first, Sadat had a hard time gaining credibility as a statesman in the eyes of the Egyptian people. Sadat was known mainly for his loyalty to Nasser. People thought that Sadat was only Nasser's yes-man. They were unsure of what Sadat could do to help Egypt. Although Sadat always maintained that he was continuing Nasser's policies, in reality his rule was quite different from Nasser's. Egypt saw nothing like the Committee of the Liquidation of Feudalism under Sadat's rule.

Two days after his election, Sadat appointed Dr. Mahmoud Fawzi as prime minister and Abdel Muhsin Abu el-Nour as secretary-general of the leftist Arab Socialist Union. He also chose his vice president, Ali Sabri, who was the leader of the Arab Socialist Union. This union could have posed a threat to Sadat's presidency, so it was a crafty move to make Sabri the vice president. The group would not threaten Sadat's rule with Sabri so close to the highest power. Sadat's thinking was that having Sabri in such an influential governmental position would take care of the group's political agenda. Sadat turned out to be a much more crafty and

■ Sadat believed that improving Egypt's strength and prosperity were vital to showing other Arab nations his concern for their own well-being. Here he meets with Amir Badr Seif El Islam of Yemen in 1970 during the Islamic Congress, a meeting of Muslim leaders.

savvy politician. Once Sabri became the vice president, Sadat proceeded to ignore all of his advice.

From the beginning, Sadat had a big challenge in ruling Egypt. When he dismissed two key ministers in the presidential cabinet, the whole cabinet resigned. The resigning cabinet members hoped that this would bring Sadat's presidency crashing to a halt. However, Sadat was unfazed. He simply used the opportunity to put the people he wanted into important cabinet positions.

Despite the challenges, Sadat was optimistic about the presidency. He wrote later in his autobiography, "I proceeded from the ideals I had always adopted, inspired by my love of Egypt and my desire to make the country a happy one. Never had I had a better chance of putting my principles into practice than when the people elected me president."

The Challenge of Leadership

Sadat faced challenges in almost every area of his government. The military was in trouble. It had not yet recovered from the Six-Day War nearly three years before. Likewise, the government needed a complete overhaul in domestic policy. Sadat had discovered that many of Nasser's officials had not been acting out of a regard for the Egyptian people. They had merely been working for their own financial and social benefit. Many of Nasser's policies had to be changed.

Sadat also realized that, after the 1956 war, Nasser had not restored the basic rights of the Egyptian people. Instead, Sadat found, Nasser had cultivated fear. He had taken over the media and eliminated the free press

■ Sadat's early successes with the Egyptian people would carry him far during subsequent difficult political times. He promoted land reform and gave farms back to the people. He vowed to reinstate the civil rights that Nasser had taken away.

in Egypt. Travel abroad was forbidden. Sadat vowed to change these things.

Egypt's economy was also in trouble. Egypt under Nasser was technically a Socialist country, meaning that the workers worked their farms for the good of the state. Free enterprise—owning one's own business—had virtually come to a standstill. The people had come to rely on the state for everything, including food, work, housing, and education. When Sadat came to power, he found that Egypt was on the verge of economic collapse. There was no foreign financial aid coming in at all. The rest of the world was letting Egypt sink or swim on its own. Nasser had thought this was good for Egypt. And it had been. But times had changed, and Sadat saw that his country could not survive much longer without gaining business deals—and getting loans—from the outside world.

Sadat's Plans for Egypt

Sadat summoned his minister of finance. The finance minister told him that the country was almost bankrupt. Nonetheless, just two months after his election, Sadat lifted all state custodianship of private property. He gave the land back to the people.

Instead of panicking about Egypt's position, Sadat focused on what he considered to be the most important task at hand: to wipe out the disgrace from the defeat in the Six-Day War. He dismantled the Arab Socialist Union. He also declared that the presidency would be a onetime, six-year term. This announcement relieved people's fear that Sadat was interested in becoming a dictator. Sadat gained much confidence from these few early moves. Of course, he was a smart politician and ruler. His experience as public relations minister worked to his advantage as he built his image in the minds of the Egyptian people. He went on the radio to talk to Egyptian citizens. He explained to them that he was raised in a small village and considered the family unit and village life sacred.

Probably the most important question Sadat would have to answer had to do with his position concerning Israel. Would he advocate another war on Israel? Egypt was in negotiations with the United Nations concerning this very issue. At the moment, Egypt and Israel remained in a cease-fire, but not many people thought this would last forever. Some decision was required. In January 1971, Sadat called a meeting of his top government officials, including the minister of war and the foreign minister. The objective was to find out what the government would do about Israel, which still held the Sinai Peninsula after the Six-Day War. Most of the government officials agreed that Egypt should go to war with Israel to get control of the land Egypt had lost.

The government also sorely needed to address its relations with the outside world. There was no real working foreign ministry, no properly thought-out policy. The Soviet Union was the only country Egypt could consider an ally. The Soviets had always shown Egypt that it was more interested in furthering its own interests in the Middle East than actually having an alliance with Egypt. In 1971, Egypt was having serious problems with the Soviets.

Egypt-Soviet Relations—and Deals

Sadat made a trip to the Soviet Union to try to repair the ruptured relations. It was a secret trip. After much negotiation, some points were hammered out. Egypt didn't want Soviet soldiers to fight Egypt's battles. Also, Egypt agreed never to initiate a confrontation between the Soviet Union and the United States. The Soviets agreed to deliver the weapons Egypt had been promised, although they did not give Egypt the exact weapons Egypt had asked for. Egypt was so desperate for weapons that Sadat said he would be willing to accept whatever weapons the Soviets wanted to give. The Russians said they would send missile-equipped aircraft and would train Egyptians to use them on one condition: that the aircraft would be used only when Soviet permission had been granted. Sadat was outraged. An agreement was eventually reached in which the Soviets promised to send aircraft, but the aircraft never arrived.

At the time, there were already four Soviet aircraft in Egypt. Sadat ordered them grounded: they could not be flown for any reason. His plan was to force the Soviets either to take

■ The only way Sadat saw to help his country avert bankruptcy was to do business with the Soviet Union. The Soviets had previously helped finance the Aswan High Dam. Now Egypt needed both military and financial aid. Here Sadat meets with Soviet general secretary Leonid Brezhnev in 1971.

the aircraft back or to agree to sell them to Egypt. Unknown to Sadat, the aircraft were there to carry out reconnaissance missions for the Soviet Fifth Fleet against the U.S. Sixth Fleet in the Mediterranean. The Soviets refused to sell the aircraft, and Sadat sent them back to Russia. "I've turned them down because of the strings attached—namely, that I should seek Moscow's approval before using them," he told the Egyptian people. This act made Sadat a few enemies within his own government.

Dealing with Israel

On February 4, 1971, Sadat announced that he would work to recover the land Egypt had lost during the Six-Day War. He also noted that the cease-fire would be extended for six months if Israel withdrew its forces from the Suez Canal. More important for the region, Sadat also offered to restore a diplomatic relationship with the United States and sign a peace agreement with Israel. For this, he wished to seek the help of the secretary-general of the United Nations.

This was the first time in twenty-two years that an Arab leader had made such a declaration. Sadat had

■ Soviet-made missiles are carried atop launch vehicles past Cairo's Unknown Soldier Memorial. Sadat used the Communist government's military hardware in Egypt's attack against Israel in 1973. Sadat wanted to finally avenge past losses against the Jewish state.

surprised all his government opponents. They had no idea what his policy would be until he announced it. Few people thought it was a good idea. Many Egyptians still felt humiliated by the outcome of the Six-Day War, and Sadat's offer of peace was looked on by many as a sign of weakness. However, Sadat knew that Egypt did not have the military power or the weapons to win a war with Israel. Unfortunately, Israel rejected Egypt's offer of peace. The United States supported Israel's decision.

CHAPTER FIVE

THE YOM KIPPUR WAR

■ An Israeli soldier leads blindfolded Egyptian soldiers captured during the 1973 Yom Kippur War. Sadat's decision to attack Israel led to both sides' realization that peace must finally be found between the two countries.

S adat called 1971 "the year of decision." However, he kept extending the deadline for the cease-fire with Israel. It was turning into a year of not very decisive action at all. In the meantime, the domestic situation was worsening. Much of the population was unemployed. There were problems with overcrowding. Of those Egyptians who did have jobs, many went on strike in protest of the situation. Prominent religious groups such as the Coptic Christians and the Muslim fundamentalists were fighting. University students demonstrated in the streets. They were fed up with Sadat's continued control of the media.

Sadat's only concession was to grant students the right to travel abroad. He did nothing more to help change the situation in Egypt. Sadat continued to censor the media because he did not want people to know how bad things really were in Egypt. Things got so bad that Sadat even closed the universities in 1972. Worse, he had many of the country's writers and intellectuals arrested on the grounds of conspiracy to overthrow the government. Egyptians were calling for war with Israel, but Sadat knew that Egypt was not ready for war. The Soviets were still procrastinating about sending weapons to Egypt. Finally, Sadat got fed up and ordered all Soviet military experts in Egypt to leave their bases and leave Egypt.

Then Sadat announced that Egypt was ready to act on America's behalf when dealing with other Arab nations. It seemed that Sadat would be throwing in his lot with the United States. He hoped that the Americans, unlike the Soviets, would send prompt military aid. Sadat knew that the United States was already sending aid to Israel. This move made Sadat popular in Egypt. The year 1973 saw Sadat trying to mend his relations with Jordan. He also pardoned many of the intellectuals he had arrested the year before.

The Yom Kippur War

On October 6, 1973, the Egyptians won an important battle in a new war against Israel. The attack took place on Yom Kippur—the Day of Atonement—which is the holiest day in the Jewish calendar. The Egyptian military began its attack by crossing the Suez Canal. It struck at military targets in the Israeli-controlled Sinai. A total of 222 aircraft completed the first wave of the battle and accomplished their mission in twenty minutes. Egypt lost only five aircraft, but Sadat lost something infinitely more precious: his nephew was killed in the conflict. No one told Sadat at the time, knowing he would be heartbroken. Sadat had virtually brought the boy up, and they were very close.

The air strike was successful, hitting 90 percent of its targets. These included command posts, combat headquarters, and centers that held electronic-warfare equipment. It took Israel, and the world, completely by surprise. Israel lost many troops in the Sinai. Lines of communication between the forces there were cut off completely. In this one air strike, the Egyptian air force recovered what it had lost in the 1956 war and the defeat in 1967 during the Six-Day War. As Sadat described that first day of battle in his autobiography, "It paved the way for our armed forces subsequently to achieve that victory which restored the self confidence of our armed forces, our people, and our Arab nation. It also restored the world's confidence in us, and exploded forever the myth of an invincible Israel."

At the same time, Syrian forces fought the Israelis in the Golan Heights. The Golan sat on the border between the two countries. Syria and Israel had often fought over the area. Other Arab nations, such as Iraq and Libya, also joined the fighting. Egyptians were celebrating their victory, but meanwhile Israel was fighting back. In four days, the Israelis drove the Syrians out of the Golan Heights. Then the Israelis sneaked across the Suez Canal and battled with the Egyptian forces. The Israelis managed to capture the western bank of the canal. This cut the Egyptians off from troop reinforcement or rescue. Sadat also refused to send reinforcements. Things looked grim for Egypt.

Then Saudi Arabia stepped in. Its action turned out to be economic rather than military. King Faisal of Saudi Arabia was tired of seeing the almost unlimited aid that the United States gave to Israel, while giving Saudi Arabia almost no help at all. On October 17, Saudi Arabia and other oil producers in the region announced that they would cut back oil production by 5 percent for all those Western countries that supported Israel. The United States was concerned but did not stop giving aid to Israel. In fact, the Americans

■ Sadat ventured to the front lines in the Sinai desert during the 1973 war. Early victories against unprepared Israeli defenses turned to stunning defeats. Israel's army quickly regrouped and pounded Egyptian forces back across the Sinai.

increased aid to Israel. This angered Saudi Arabia so much that the Saudis increased their cutbacks on oil production.

The crisis became serious enough that other countries, namely the Soviet Union, began to worry that the situation was escalating out of control. Sadat, whose troops began to lose, asked the Soviets to sponsor a cease-fire resolution in the United Nations. Although the Soviets did just that, Israel kept on fighting and reversing Arab successes until a United Nations emergency force arrived in the area to supervise a cease-fire.

After the Yom Kippur War

In 1971, Sadat had offered peace to Israel, and Israel had refused, supported by the United States. After the 1973 Yom Kippur War, it seemed clear to everyone that peace between Egypt and Israel was in everyone's best interests—even the interests of the United States. The Yom Kippur War made Israeli-Arab tensions very clear. Israel just wanted to be recognized as a sovereign country and wanted to live in peace with the Arab nations. The Arab world wanted

■ Sadat's generals look on as Sadat reviews a map showing the latest troop movements. Sadat learned that starting a war to help the economy was not always the best decision. People on the home front were awaiting a victory that never came.

Israel to return the Gaza Strip and the Sinai Peninsula. Also, the Arabs wanted East Jerusalem to be returned to their hands. The Palestinians needed their own state, one that Israel would recognize.

It would be years before peace was attained. Egypt and Sadat had a long way to endure. Sadat needed to deal with the immediate effects of the Yom Kippur War. Although Egypt had an initial stunning victory during the Yom Kippur War, conditions were as bad as ever at home. The expense of the war made the Egyptian economy even worse. As is often the case, countries would ask their allies for help in rebuilding their economy after a war. Sadat had few allies left, however. He had alienated the Soviet Union by asking its military experts to leave Egypt. And other Arab nations, such as Syria, were unhappy that Egypt had agreed to a cease-fire with Israel.

Saving Egypt's Economy

Sadat decided to initiate programs to improve Egypt's economy. First, he wanted more of Egypt's major businesses to be run by private investors. This was directly opposite to the

■ Sadat's choice to sign a cease-fire agreement with Israel brought him appreciation from world leaders. United States president Richard Nixon is shown during his visit to Cairo in 1974. The United States became involved with the Middle East peace process that continues to this day.

way Nasser had run the country. Under Nasser, much of the business in Egypt had been organized and run by the state. Sadat tried to get foreign investors to put money into Egyptian enterprises by pointing out that cheap labor was readily available in Egypt. Also, he suggested that the government would not put heavy taxes on new businesses.

Sadat's efforts did little more than widen the already incredible economic gulf between the rich and the poor. Some money did go for new real estate projects. This move made money for the government but forced the poor back onto farmlands that could no longer support them. New farming laws established in 1975 resulted in many of the peasants losing land. People knew Sadat had been born into a farming family in the little village of Mit Abul Kum. Now many Egyptian farmers felt that he had betrayed them with his new policies.

The solution seemed clear, but it was not easy to accomplish. How would Sadat begin to broach a relationship with America and still keep Arab unity? Many Arab nations did not want to deal with the United States because it recognized and supported Israel. The Arabs, angered by the plight of the Palestinian Arabs, did not recognize Israel and preferred not to deal with any country that did recognize it. The Arabs were particularly angered by states that also supported Israel.

America now seemed interested in pursuing peace with Arab nations. King Faisal of Saudi Arabia still would not increase oil exports. The United Nations set up a conference in 1973 to discuss peace in the Middle East. Israel agreed to get out of the eastern bank of the Suez Canal. Israel signed a cease-fire treaty in 1974, and

■ Sadat enjoyed mass appeal throughout the Arab world for Sadat's attacks on Israel. He took this opportunity to reopen the Suez Canal. Tolls to use the canal were added to help Egypt recover from its economic woes.

United States president Richard Nixon visited Egypt and Israel that same year. Sadat was delighted. The United States continued to negotiate with Israel to withdraw from the Sinai territory. Then Sadat did a daring thing.

Reopening the Suez Canal

Sadat reopened the Suez Canal in June 1975. This was a daring move because the Israeli army still sat within shooting range. The canal had been closed since June 1967, and Egypt had suffered terrible financial losses

Menachem Begin

Menachem Begin was born in Brast-Litovsk, Russia, in 1913. The fighting of the German and Russian armies during World War I (1914–1918) forced many families, including Begin's, to leave Russia for a safer place to live.

Begin was a Zionist. Zionism was a movement that embraced the idea of Jews returning to Palestine and claiming their ancient homeland. As early as his teens, Begin was taking on leadership roles in Zionist groups. By 1936, he was leading a group in Czechoslovakia. By 1938, he was the head of a group in Poland that boasted 100,000 members. The group was dedicated to defending Jews in Poland, and its purpose loomed ever larger as the first stirrings of Nazi anti-Semitism rumbled through Europe. The group's members were completely trained in the use of weapons. Begin was imprisoned in Siberia in 1940 but was set free in 1941 when the Nazis invaded the Soviet Union, because Begin was a Polish citizen. He joined the Free Polish Army, which in 1943 went to Palestine, at that time controlled by Britain. From 1943 to 1948, Begin belonged to the guerrilla-terrorist Zionist group Irgun Zvai Leumi (National Military Organization). The group plotted to overthrow Britain in Palestine. The Jewish state of Israel was created in 1948, and Irgun Zvai Leumi was no longer necessary.

Begin held various government positions, such as head of the Freedom Party, from 1948 until he was elected prime minister of Israel in 1977. He won the Nobel Peace Prize with Anwar Sadat for Israel's peace with Egypt, symbolized by the Camp David Accords.

Menachem Begin became the Israeli prime minister in 1977. He did not trust Anwar Sadat's call for peace talks. Sadat had been part of three wars against Israel. Begin stepped lightly toward the peace negotiations table.

because of it. Israel agreed to leave another part of the Sinai Peninsula in 1975, on some conditions. First, the United States would have to send up-to-date military equipment to Israel. Second, the United States would not negotiate with the Palestine Liberation Organization (PLO) until the PLO recognized Israel. Third, Egypt had to agree to remain neutral if Israel and Syria went to war.

Meanwhile, things in Egypt were still in the same fix. Riots broke out in 1977 when, under pressure from the International Monetary Fund, Sadat cut the government subsidies on the food items that the poor most needed, such as bread and beans. For thirty-six hours, Egyptian cities were mob scenes. Sadat had his police arrest many people. He decided that now more than ever was the time to try to convince the United States to give Egypt the kind of aid that Israel had been given.

Easing Tensions and Getting Help from Neighbors

Some Arab nations began to send money to Egypt in an effort to prevent trouble in the Middle East. They were still not happy about Sadat's

■ On November 20, 1977, Sadat and Begin sat for a press conference. The Egyptian president's official visit to Jerusalem was the first time an Arab leader had met to negotiate peace with Israel. Sadat's move toward peace would gain him many enemies in the Arab world.

cease-fire with Israel, but they could no longer turn their backs on a fellow Arab nation. The United States also sent money: $200 million. All of this was not enough to get Egypt's economy to recover. Sadat made another daring leap.

In early 1977, Sadat announced that he would go anywhere—even into the Israeli Knesset (parliament)—to make peace with Israel. Nothing of the kind had been announced in Egypt before. No one was sure how to take Sadat's statement. The Egyptian press debated whether it was a good idea. The Israelis weren't sure whether to take Sadat seriously. Israeli's prime minister, Menachem Begin, didn't trust Anwar Sadat. The United States thought peace was a great idea and welcomed Sadat's peaceful sentiments. Everyone was surprised when Menachem Begin sent Sadat an invitation to speak in the Israeli Knesset. Sadat went to Jerusalem in November 1977.

CHAPTER SIX

PEACE WITH ISRAEL

■ Sadat acknowledges the Israeli flag during ceremonies in Tel Aviv in 1977. Sadat used his media image to build trust in the peace process with Israel. He knew that Egypt needed peace in order to draw goodwill, financial aid, and business deals with the West.

S adat was the first Egyptian leader to visit Israel since the time of Cleopatra (69–30 BC). Sadat's visit had a great impact in the media. He understood that his media image would be of great importance for Egypt then and in the future. It would influence how the world saw Egypt. A positive media image for Sadat would signal to the world that Egypt was a modern country and one to be respected.

The countries of the world had differing reactions to Sadat's visit. The United States supported this action. Syria, however, another Arab-Muslim country, thought Sadat's choice was terrible and foolish. The Syrian government actually declared official mourning.

Whatever the reaction by different heads of state, Sadat's visit was a historically dramatic gesture. It was pivotal in starting the process of peace between Egypt and Israel and between the other countries of the Middle East. It was not an easy gesture to give and, once given, not an easy task in which to succeed.

Sadat learned, once he had begun talks with Israel, that peace would not come easily. When he returned to Egypt, he felt victorious although no agreement had been signed. Something had changed because of Sadat's visit, though. The United States was more determined than ever to help Egypt and Israel work out their differences. In 1978, United States president Jimmy Carter invited President Sadat and Prime Minister Begin to Camp David in Maryland for peace talks. Both of the leaders accepted.

The Camp David Accords

For a while, the peace talks were slow going. At first, Begin was not willing to talk about Israel withdrawing from any of the territory it had won in previous wars. Then he came around to the idea of withdrawing from the Sinai Peninsula but not from the Gaza Strip, the Golan Heights, or the West Bank. He said that he would submit the idea to the Israeli parliament. After thirteen

■ Three world leaders—Anwar Sadat, Jimmy Carter, and Menachem Begin—meet at Camp David, Maryland, at the start of peace talks. Brokering peace between the Arab and Jewish countries would not be an easy task.

days of talking, everyone went home after writing drafts of two peace agreements, called the Camp David Accords. The accords had not yet been signed, but at least some moves toward peace had been put down on paper.

Menachem Begin and Anwar Sadat were awarded the Nobel Peace Prize in 1978 for their efforts, even though the Camp David agreements had not yet been signed. Begin went to Sweden to accept the award, but Sadat did not. Sadat stayed home, in part because the other Arab nations were not happy with Egypt's separate peace with Israel.

The Arab nations met in November 1978 to decide how to react to Egypt's Camp David Accords. They offered to pay Sadat 2.5 billion Egyptian pounds per year if he wouldn't sign the peace treaties. Sadat refused the offer.

There was a controversy between Israel and Egypt over several details. In March 1979, Carter visited both Egypt and Israel to try to make the Camp David agreements work. Oil was one of the issues about which Israel was worried. Begin worried that if Israel withdrew from the Sinai Peninsula, with its rich oil fields, there might be a problem meeting energy needs. It was written into the treaty that Egypt would supply oil to Israel. Jimmy Carter also promised that the United States would supply oil for the next fifteen years if Israel had trouble getting it. On March 26, 1979, the three leaders met on the lawn of the White House and signed the treaty.

Many people were happy that peace had been achieved, but not everyone was. The unavoidable fact was that Egypt had created a sepa-rate peace with Israel. Doing so cost Egypt its place in the Arab League. In addition, the Arab countries canceled

■ Peace between Israel and Egypt became a process of assuring border rights, oil sales, and a nonaggression pact. For all the smiles in front of the cameras, the three leaders were not always agreeable in private. Tense moments at Camp David almost ruined the chance for peace in the Middle East.

their aid to Egypt. Saudi Arabia did not give Egypt the aircraft that had been promised. American aid was beginning to look like the best bet for Egypt. In 1980, however, Jimmy Carter lost the presidential election to Ronald Reagan. Sadat was unsure whether the United States, under its new president, would continue to be so receptive to helping Egypt.

Befriending the United States

Sadat did several things to help continue his good relations with the United States. He gave aid to several countries whose governments were backed by the United States, including selling weapons to Somalia. Sadat's confidence in America was not misplaced. Egypt received more help from America than ever. The U.S. Embassy in Egypt came to be staffed by hundreds of people and was moved to a new, bigger building.

This sort of progress came with a price: the Muslim fundamentalists criticized Sadat for his alliance with the West. And Sadat's policies of the last several years had angered more and more of the Muslim fundamentalist community. The fundamentalists believed that Sadat was betraying Islamic law by being so controlling. For instance, after his reelection in 1976, Sadat had made himself president for life. This contributed to the unrest that Egypt was experiencing because of continued problems with the economy, inflation, and overcrowding. Sadat responded by making laws that gave him the right to shut people out of public life who came under suspicion of working against or speaking against the government. Then, in 1980, Sadat passed a law that was known as the Law

■ Two years after Sadat made public his wish for peace, a treaty was signed between Egypt and Israel. President Carter looks on in front of the White House as Sadat and Begin sign the many documents that have kept the peace between the two countries since March 26, 1979.

of Shame. It amounted to censorship of anyone who did not express the prevailing views of the government. Sadat thought these laws were needed to curb unrest. They did this up to a point. Then people's anger spilled over.

In the summer of 1981, riots broke out in Cairo between the Coptic Christians and the fundamentalist Muslims. Sadat took the opportunity to arrest 1,500 people who just happened not to agree with his legislation. Many Muslim fundamentalists were in this group.

Assassination

Since Egypt's victory in the Yom Kippur War (1973), Sadat had held a military parade every year to commemorate that event. No one in Egypt could forget that, during the Yom Kippur War, Egypt had launched a surprise attack, sneaked across the Suez Canal, and regained land that Egypt had lost during the humiliating Six-Day War.

Sadat enjoyed dressing in his military uniform and sitting in the review stand to watch the tanks, jeeps, and soldiers pass by. On October 6, 1981, Sadat sat in the review stand as usual. His wife, Jehan, was attended by bodyguards to a place behind Sadat, in a glassed-in area for her protection. The parade progressed as usual. Then, suddenly, one of the jeeps stopped in front of Sadat. Soldiers came out of the jeep and pointed guns at Sadat. The soldiers sprayed Sadat with bursts of automatic gunfire. Sadat collapsed as Hosni Mubarak, vice president of Egypt, looked on in horror. The assassins got away from the scene, taking advantage of the shock and confusion. They were Muslim fundamentalists who

■ The aftermath of Anwar Sadat's assassination is shown in the chaos atop the review stand in Cairo on October 6, 1981. Sadat's enemies used his signing of the Camp David Accords as reason enough to kill him.

were part of a group in Sadat's army that opposed his policies. They felt, as did many Muslim fundamentalists, that Sadat had betrayed them.

Much of the world mourned Sadat's death, including Europe and the United States. Many Arab states were not sad that Sadat was gone. Three former U.S. presidents, Jimmy Carter, Gerald Ford, and Richard Nixon, attended Sadat's funeral. The Arab nations were not well represented there. Only dignitaries from Somalia, Sudan, and Oman attended. Sadat was buried in a small cemetery outside Cairo.

Sadat's Legacy

Anwar Sadat's story is more than a rags-to-riches story. He saw a purpose to his rise from a poor peasant family through the military to become Egypt's president. Although he lived a fabulously wealthy lifestyle as president, Sadat believed his village life was always an important part of him. In this, he felt close to United States president Jimmy Carter, saying, "He is a farmer, like me."

Sadat was an ambitious man who, all his life, did whatever it took to accomplish his goals. This included revolutionary activity that got him imprisoned. It also included radically reevaluating his belief that Israel should not be recognized as a country. In reexamining his view of Israel, Sadat took the first step to achieving peace with Israel. Sadat had a brave vision that brought about peace and ultimately his death.

A reporter once asked Sadat what he would wish for, if given three wishes. Sadat responded, "Peace in the Middle East. Peace in the Middle East. Peace in the Middle

■ The Egyptian prime minister accepts the Nobel Peace Prize that Anwar Sadat earned in 1978 following Egypt's peace treaty with Israel. The other Arab and Islamic countries of the region still regard Israel as an enemy.

East." It is certain that Sadat devoted much of his energy and all of his political skill to the cause of peace in the Middle East. The poor peasant from Mit Abul Kum, son of the effendi, and one of thirteen children, achieved his dreams of seeing his beloved Egypt free from Britain's colonialism. Sadat wanted to make Egypt a modern country, and he succeeded in the way that he used the power of image to make peace with Israel. It is a distinctly modern political strategy to create one's public image via the media, and that is exactly what Sadat did.

■ Anwar Sadat is honored to this day as a great leader within Egypt and around the world. His legacy is a lasting peace between two nations in an area that today continues to see wars and killing.

Sadat was a complex man whose policies were not always easy to figure out. As a key member of Nasser's government, Sadat was so loyal to Nasser that he was nicknamed Colonel Yes. Yet when Sadat took over the presidency after Nasser's death, he undid many of the economic policies that Nasser had put into effect. Sadat may be best remembered as the Egyptian leader whose speech before the Israeli parliament electrified the world. He stood before the Knesset and said, "I declare it to the whole world, that we accept to live with you in permanent peace based on justice."

1918 Anwar el-Sadat is born in Mit Abul Kum on December 25.

1925 Sadat family moves to town near Cairo; Anwar attends a private school called the Islamic Benevolent Society School.

1930 Sadat earns primary education certificate and enrolls in Fuad I Secondary School.

1936 Sadat enters the Royal Military Academy.

1938 Sadat graduates from the academy and marries a woman chosen by his parents.

1939 Sadat helps to found the Free Officers Organization.

1942 Sadat is imprisoned for working secretly with the German army.

1948 Sadat divorces his first wife; he is implicated in the assassination of Amin Osman Pasha and is sent to jail for a second time.

1949 Sadat leaves the military after prison and marries for a second time.

1950 Sadat reenters the military.

1951 Sadat promoted to lieutenant colonel but keeps a low profile in politics and with the Free Officers.

1952 Sadat announces on July 23 that King Farouk has been overthrown. The Free Officers are renamed the Revolutionary Command Council. Sadat is made minister of state in the new government.

1954 Sadat works with the British military during transition of rule over the Suez Canal Zone.

1956	The Suez Canal War.
1958	Egypt and Syria found the United Arab Republic (UAR).
1962	Syria withdraws from the UAR.
1967	The Six-Day War is fought between Egypt and Israel.
1969	Sadat is promoted to vice president of Egypt.
1970	Nasser dies. Sadat is elected president of Egypt.
1971	Sadat offers a peace treaty to Israel, which is rejected.
1973	The Third Arab-Israeli War, called the Yom Kippur War.
1977	Sadat visits Jerusalem for peace talks with Menachem Begin.
1978	Peace negotiations between Egypt and Israel at Camp David.
1979	The Camp David Accords.
1981	Sadat is assassinated by a fundamentalist Muslim group.

allies Countries that are friendly and help each other in a time of crisis.

assassination The killing of an important person.

canal A channel cut from one waterway to another to allow passage of boats or ships.

cease-fire A military order to stop fighting.

colonialism The system by which a country maintains foreign colonies.

Coptic Descendant of the ancient people of Egypt, now Christian.

crucial Necessary.

delta The earth and sand that collect at the mouth of a river.

destiny A course of events that is determined before the outcome.

feudalism An ancient system in which people worked and fought for a landowner who gave them small pieces of land to work and protected them.

fugitive Someone on the run from the law.

fundamentalist Having to do with a strict interpretation of religious writings or beliefs.

invincible Not able to be harmed.

irrigate To divert a water source, such as a lake or river, and use it to water crops.

Koran The Muslim holy book.

Muslim A follower of the Islamic religion.

nationalism A strong feeling of pride for one's country.

Nazi A member of the German army under the leadership of Adolf Hitler.

oppressive Having to do with the unjust use of power over another.

parliament A group that makes a country's laws.

pasha A man of high rank or office in Turkey and parts of North Africa.

peaceful revolution Changing government control through nonviolent action.

premier A political leader.

prime minister The leader of a government.

revolutionary New or very different.

Organizations

Amnesty International
322 8th Avenue
New York, NY 10001
(212) 807-8400
e-mail: admin-us@aiusa.org
Web site: http://www.amnestyusa.org

Arab Organization for Human Rights
91 Al-Marghany Street
Heliopolis
Cairo, Egypt
e-mail: aohr@link.com.eg
Web site: http://www.aohr.org

Center for Arab Unity Studies
Lyon Street-Sadat Tower Bldg.
P.O. Box Hamra Beirut 1103 2090
Beirut, Lebanon
Web site: http://www.caus.org.lb

Council on American-Islamic Relations (CAIR)
453 New Jersey Avenue SE
Washington, DC 20003
(202) 488-8787
Web site: http://www.cair-net.org

Egyptian Organization for Human Rights
8/10 Mathaf El-Manial Street, 10th Floor
Manyal El-roda
Cairo, Egypt
(202) 363-6811 or 362-0467
Web site: http://www.eohr.org.eg

Middle East Studies Association of North America
c/o The University of Arizona
1643 E. Helen Street
Tucson, AZ 85721
(520) 621-5850
e-mail: mesana@u.arizona.edu
Web site: http://w3fp.arizona.edu/mesassoc

Web Sites

Due to the changing nature of Internet links, the Rosen Publishing Group, Inc., has developed an online list of Web sites related to the subject of this book. This site is updated regularly. Please use this link to access the list:

http://www.rosenlinks.com/mel/asad

Beattie, Kirk J. *Egypt During the Sadat Years.* New York: Palgrave Macmillan, 2000.

Finke, Blythe Foote. *Anwar Sadat: Egyptian Ruler and Peace Maker.* New York: Story House Corp., 1987.

Israeli, Raphael. *Man of Defiance: A Political Biography of Anwar Sadat.* New York: Barnes & Noble, 1985.

Kras, Sarah Louise. *Anwar Sadat.* Philadelphia: Chelsea House, 2000.

Sadat, Anwar. *Those I Have Known.* New York: Continuum Publishing Group, 1984.

Sadat, Camelia. *My Father and I.* New York: Macmillan, 1985.

BIBLIOGRAPHY

Aufderheide, Patricia, ed. *Anwar Sadat.*
   Philadelphia: Chelsea House, 1989.
Sadat, Anwar. *In Search of Identity: An Autobiography.*
   New York: HarperCollins, 1978.

INDEX

A

Alexandria, Egypt, 28, 32, 34, 44
Arab nations, 5, 36, 47, 54, 74, 78–80, 82, 86–88, 90, 91, 92–94
Aswan High Dam, 28, 46, 47
Atatürk, Kemal, 14, 16, 24

B

Begin, Menachem, 5, 84, 88, 90, 91, 92

C

Cairo, 17–18, 26, 28, 30, 32, 40, 43, 49, 51, 60, 95, 98
Camp David Accords, 84, 90–94
Carter, Jimmy, 90, 92, 94, 98
Coptic Christians, 74, 95

E

Egypt, 6, 7, 8, 10, 24, 32, 36, 90
  as a colony, 10–12, 22, 26, 28, 30, 36, 44, 99
  economy of, 66, 80–82, 88, 94, 101
  government/politics, 4, 13, 22, 26, 28, 30, 32, 36, 43–46, 47, 49, 51, 60–62, 63, 64–66, 67, 68–70, 72, 74, 80–82, 86, 88, 89–90, 94–95, 101
  media/public relations in, 43, 44, 64, 67, 74, 90, 99
  military of, 7, 14, 21, 22, 24, 28, 36, 40, 41, 42, 43, 51, 53, 54, 57, 58, 60, 64, 68–70, 72, 74, 75, 76, 78, 94, 96, 98
  people of, 5, 8, 12, 22, 32, 38, 49, 51, 62, 64, 66, 67, 70, 73–74, 76, 82, 86

uprisings and revolutions in, 11, 12, 20, 26, 28, 30, 43–44, 51, 86, 95

F

Faisal, King, 47–49, 76, 82
farmers/farming, 7, 8, 10, 12, 14, 49, 51, 82, 98
Farouk, King, 18, 28, 43, 44, 49
France, 8, 10, 11, 46, 47
Free Officers Organization, 28, 30, 32, 40, 42–43, 44

G

Gandhi, Mohandas, 14, 26
Gaza Strip, 47, 54, 80, 90
Germany/Germans, 13, 16, 30–32, 84
Golan Heights, 53, 75, 76, 90
Great Britain/British, 10–11, 12, 16, 21, 22, 26, 28, 30, 32, 34, 36, 43, 44, 46, 47, 49, 60, 84, 99

H

Hitler, Adolf, 16, 30

I

Iraq, 36, 76
Israel, 5, 34, 36, 47, 51, 53, 54, 67, 70, 72, 73, 74, 75–80, 82, 83, 84, 86, 88, 90, 99, 101

J

Jews, 34, 36, 84
Jordan/Transjordan, 36, 53, 54, 74

M

Mediterranean Sea, 8, 10, 70

110

About the Author

Magdalena Alagna is a writer and editor living and working in New York City.

Photo Credits

Front cover map, pp. 8–9, 34–35 Courtesy of the Perry-Castãnedia Library Map Collection/The University of Texas at Austin; cover image, p. 96–97 © Kevin Fleming/Corbis; back cover flags, pp. 1, 3, 4, 6, 21, 42, 58, 73, 89, 102, 104, 106, 108, 109, 110 © Nelson Sá; pp. 1, 4, 80–81, 84–85, 95 © Wally McNamee/Corbis; pp. 3 (chapter 1 and 2 box), 6, 11, 13, 14-15, 17, 21, 25, 54–55, 68–69, 73 © Hulton/Archive/Getty Images; pp. 3 (chapter 3 and 6 box), 27, 28–29, 37, 38–39, 42, 45, 50, 52–53, 56, 58, 83, 89, 91 © Bettmann/Corbis; pp. 3 (chapter 4 box), 22–23, 33, 60–61, 63, 64–65 © Hulton-Deutsch Collection/Corbis; pp. 3 (chapter 5 box), 31, 70–71, 76–77, 78–79 © AP/Wide World Photos; pp.18–19, 48–49, 92–93 © Corbis; p. 86–87 © Karel William/Corbis; p. 99 © David Rubinger/Corbis; p. 100 © Carl & Ann Purcell/Corbis.

Designer: Nelson Sá; **Editor:** Mark Beyer;
Photo Researcher: Nelson Sá